First published 2010 by North Parade Publishing Ltd.

First Racehorse for Young Readers Edition 2017

All rights to any and all materials in copyright owned by the publisher are strictly reserved by the publisher.

Racehorse for Young Readers books may be purchased in bulk at special discounts for sales promotion, corporate gifts, fund-raising, or educational purposes. Special editions can also be created to specifications. For details, contact the Special Sales Department, Skyhorse Publishing, 307 West 36th Street, 11th Floor, New York, NY 10018 or info@skyhorsepublishing.com.

Racehorse for Young Readers™ is a pending trademark of Skyhorse Publishing, Inc.®,
a Delaware corporation.

Visit our website at www.skyhorsepublishing.com.

10 9 8 7 6 5 4 3 2

Cover design by North Parade Publishing
Predominant artwork and imagery: Shutterstock

ISBN: 978-1-63158-241-7

Printed in China

My First 1000 Words

FOR YOUNG READERS

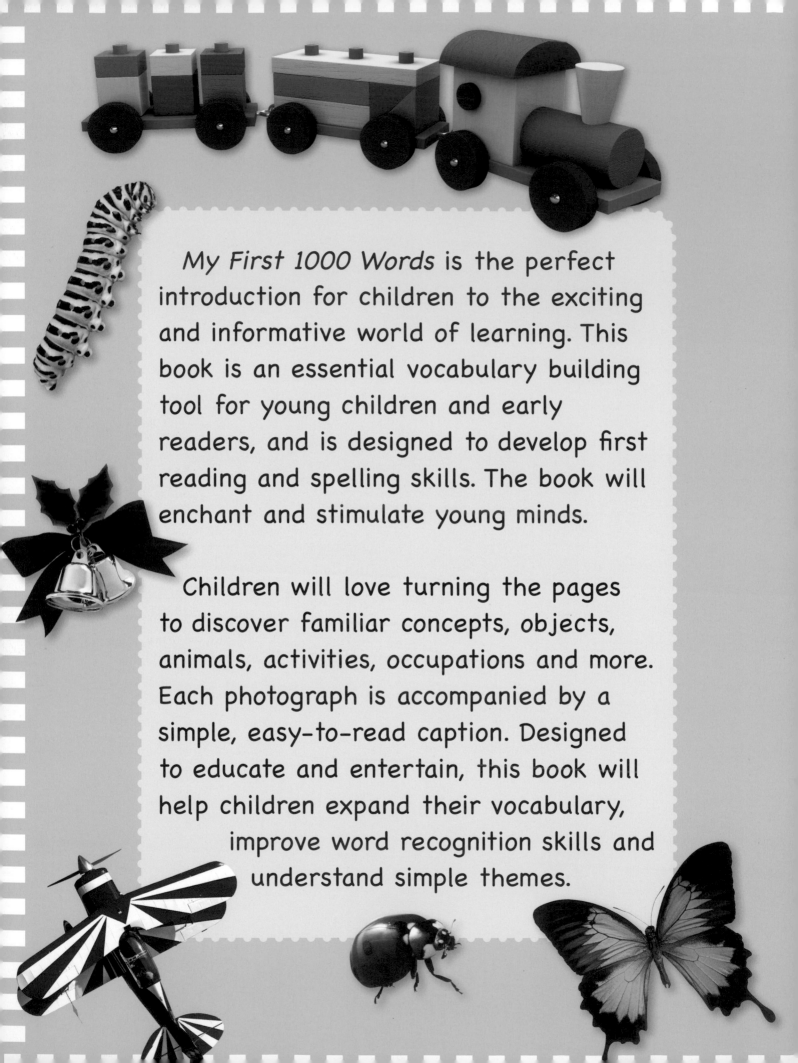

My First 1000 Words is the perfect introduction for children to the exciting and informative world of learning. This book is an essential vocabulary building tool for young children and early readers, and is designed to develop first reading and spelling skills. The book will enchant and stimulate young minds.

Children will love turning the pages to discover familiar concepts, objects, animals, activities, occupations and more. Each photograph is accompanied by a simple, easy-to-read caption. Designed to educate and entertain, this book will help children expand their vocabulary, improve word recognition skills and understand simple themes.

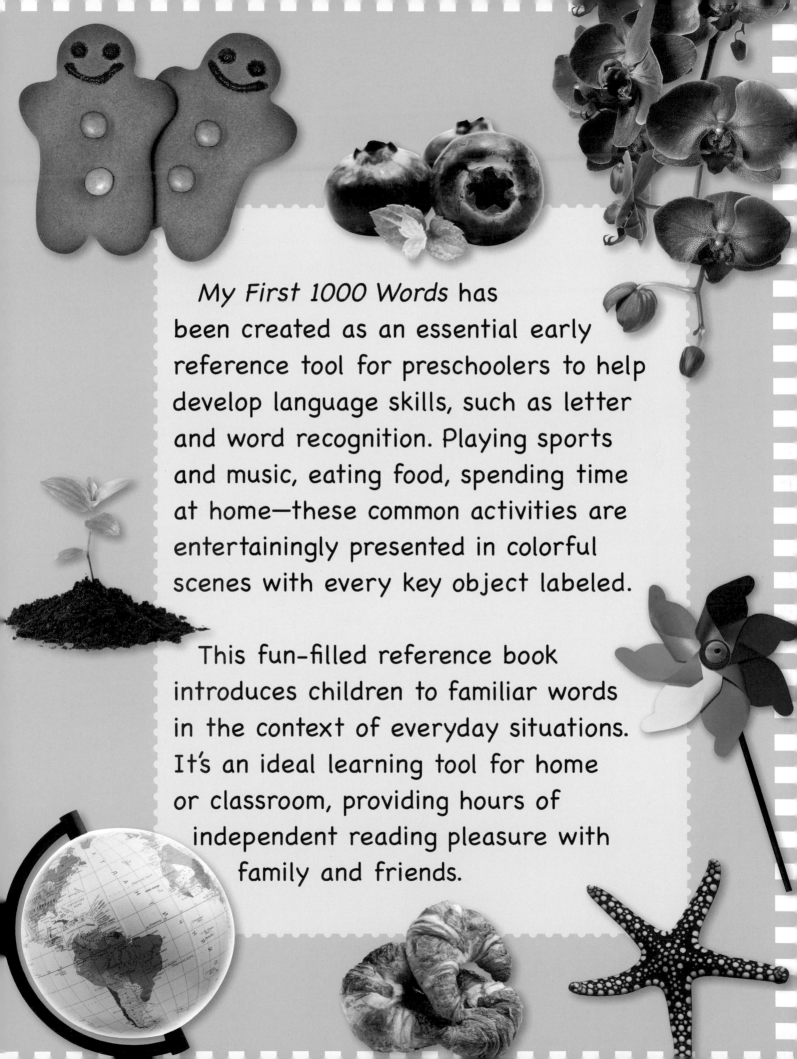

My First 1000 Words has
been created as an essential early
reference tool for preschoolers to help
develop language skills, such as letter
and word recognition. Playing sports
and music, eating food, spending time
at home—these common activities are
entertainingly presented in colorful
scenes with every key object labeled.

This fun-filled reference book
introduces children to familiar words
in the context of everyday situations.
It's an ideal learning tool for home
or classroom, providing hours of
independent reading pleasure with
family and friends.

Household Pets

These animals are found at home. Do you have any pets?

Goldfish

Parakeet

Rabbit

Dog

Mouse

Parrot

Lizard

Cat

Farm Animals

These animals live and work on and around farms and parks.

Donkey

Duck

Rooster

Pig

Goose

Sheep

Cow

Squirrel

Turkey

In the Garden

How many of these creatures have you seen in your garden?

Butterfly

Spider

Ant

Caterpillar

Starling

Bee

Robin

Ladybird

Centipede

Wasp

Moth

Snail

Grasshopper

Slug

Magpie

Green Cricket

Earthworm

In the Jungle

These are some of the wild animals that live in or near jungles.

Snake

Tiger

Hawk

Wolf

Chimpanzee

Quetzal

Sloth Bear

Monkey

Toucan

Spider Monkey

Orangutan

Macaw

Bat

Warthog

Capybara

Howler Monkey

Leopard

On the Grasslands

Some animals live on the grasslands. Let's take a look at them.

Wildebeest

Lion

Baboon

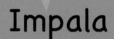
Impala

Zebra

Giraffe

Hyena

Rhinoceros

In the Mountains

The mountains are also home to several animals. Let's see what they are.

Addax

Mountain Goat

Ground Squirrel

Brown Bear

Panda

Bison

Snow Leopard

Golden Eagle

Gorilla

In the Pond

Have you looked into a pond? Did you see any of these creatures?

Frog

Dragon Fly

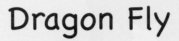

Tadpole

Mosquito

Koi Fish

Salamander

May Fly

Water Strider

Toad

In the Deserts

Animals can also be found in the deserts. Here are some of them.

Rattlesnake

Ostrich

Coyote

Dingo

Camel

Black Widow
Spider

Kangaroo

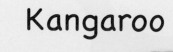

Vulture

In the Oceans

The seas are home to many creatures as well as fish.

Dolphin

Sponge

Angel Fish

Star Fish

Sting Ray

Coral

Pelican

Parrot Fish

Killer Whale

Humpback Whale

Clownfish

Seahorse

Seagull

Eel

Crab

Octopus

Great White Shark

In the Rivers

Even the rivers are teeming with wildlife and not all of them are fish.

River Turtle

Aligator

Otter

Trout

Boutu

Piranha

Anaconda

River Dolphin

At the Poles

These creatures live in the extreme cold of the poles.

Penguin

Snow Owl

Arctic Fox

Walrus

Arctic Hare

Narwhal

Polar Bear

Puffin

Seal

Good Morning

What do you do when you get up in the morning?

Toothbrush

Toothpaste

Milk

Cereal

Juice

Sugar

Spoon

Bread

Bowl

Eggs

Time for a Bath

After brushing your teeth and having breakast, it's time for a bath.

Towel

Bath Toy

Shampoo

Soap

Comb

Bathrobe

Bathtub

My Body

These are the different important parts of your body.

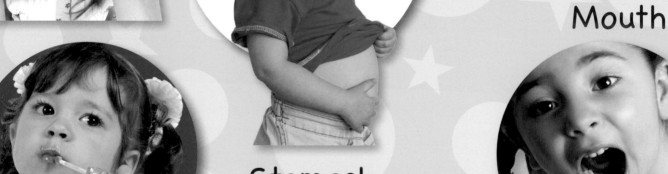

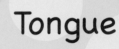

Cheek

Tongue

Mouth

Stomach

Lips

Legs

Head

Hands

Feet

Hair

Toes

Eye

Fingers

Nose

Teeth

Arm

Ear

What I Do

How many of these activities do you do everyday?

Drink

Jump

Read

Play

Smile

Cry

Sleep

Eat

My Clothes

These are the different types of clothes you wear everyday.

Gloves

Jacket

Shoes

Scarf

Socks

T-Shirt

Hat

Pants

Sweater

Around the House

These are some objects around the house. Can you name them?

Chair

Television

Door

Vacuum

Lamp

Table

Phone

Radio

Key

Window

Music Player

Sofa

Fan

Air Conditioner

Timer

Roof

Picture

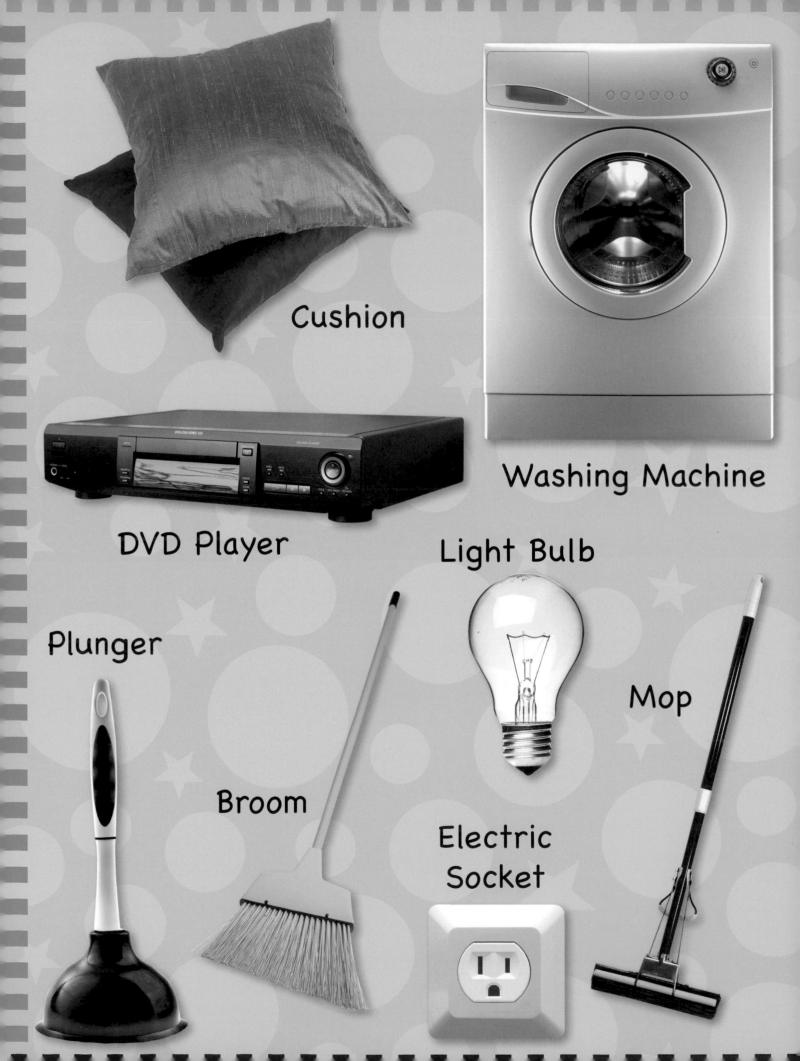

Cushion

Washing Machine

DVD Player

Light Bulb

Plunger

Mop

Broom

Electric
Socket

Laundry Basket

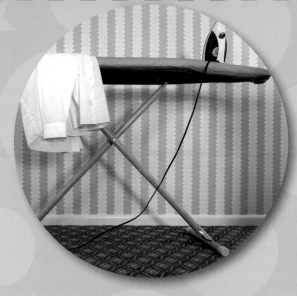

Ironing Board

Detergent
Bottle

Lock

Shaver

Wall
Switch

Electric Iron

Vase

Bathroom
Brush

Doghouse

Birdhouse

Coaster

Fire
Extinguisher

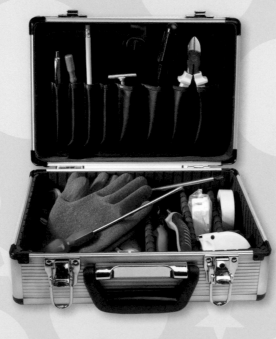

Toolbox

Umbrella
Stand

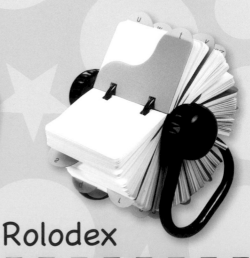

Rolodex

Candelabra

Coat Hanger

Mailbox

Curtain

Stepladder

First Aid Box

Fish Bowl

Laundry Basket

Stool

Bathmat

It's Bedtime

It's time for bed. Do you recognize these objects?

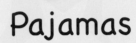

Pillow

Bed

Pajamas

Blanket

Soft Toy

Night Light

Books

Reading Lamp

Colors

How many of these colors
do you recognize?

Green Apple

Orange

Violet Flower

Yellow Flower

Red Purse

Black Hat

Blue Butterfly

Gray Bag

Purple Eggplant

Let's Play

Which of these toys would you like to play with?

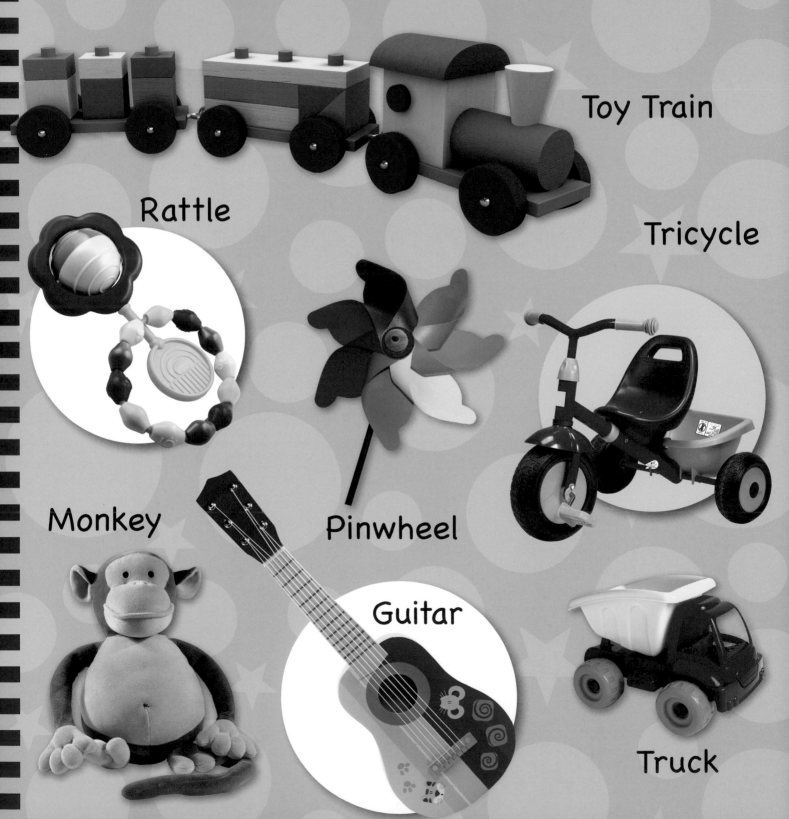

Toy Train

Rattle

Tricycle

Monkey

Pinwheel

Guitar

Truck

Toy Plane

Robot

Ball

Toy Phone

Wagon

Toy Blocks

Rocking Horse

Doll

Car

Getting Ready

Going on a trip? Let's get ready for it first.

Map

Backpack

Tickets

Passport

Compass

Suitcase

What to Pack

Let's see, what do you need to pack for the trip?

Pants

Swimming Goggles

Jacket

Sun Hat

Shirt

Sun Cream

Sandals

Sunglasses

Sweater

Shorts

Swimsuit

At the Beach

Aren't beaches fun? Have you spotted any of these objects on a beach?

Sandcastle

Palm Tree

Lifejacket

Surfboard

Shell

Hammock

Bucket

Starfish

Frisbee

Seashell

Coral

Dolphin

Life Buoy

Coral

Beach
Umbrella

Deck
Chair

Crab

Beach
Shovel

Christmas

Yay, it's Christmas time!
Time for some holiday cheer.

Turkey

Hot Chocolate

Bells

Candles

Santa Claus

Cake

Present

Angel

Cookies

Christmas Stocking

Stars

Nativity

Sleigh

Tinsel

Holly

Holly Wreath

Reindeer

Cracker

Mistletoe

Fireplace

Christmas
Hat

Gingerbread Men

Merry Christmas!
and Happy New Year!

Red Ribbon

Christmas Card

Christmas Tree

Candy
Cane

Carol Singers

Snowman

Eggnog

Christmas Decorations

Elf

Lights

Family

Chimney

Halloween

Shhh . . . it's halloween. All the ghosts and spirits are about.

Candy

Scarecrow

Costumes

Bonfire

Ghost

Skeleton

Pumpkin Pie

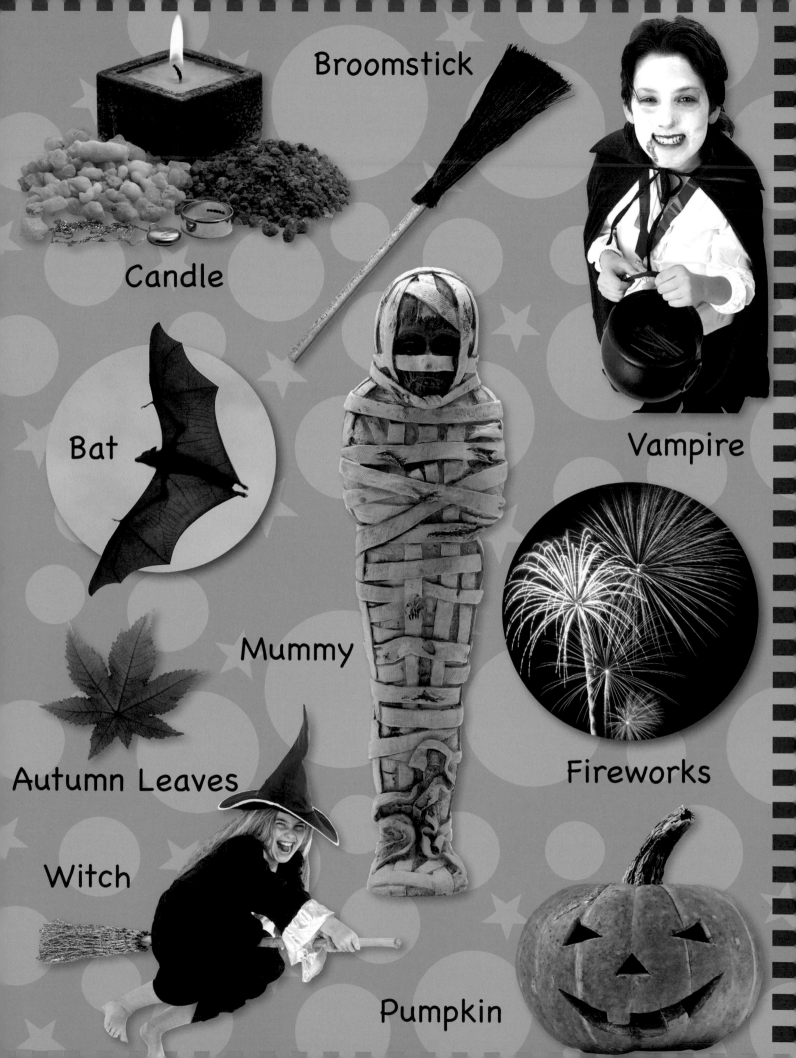

Candle

Broomstick

Vampire

Bat

Mummy

Fireworks

Autumn Leaves

Witch

Pumpkin

Easter

Easter is not just about the egg hunt, is it?

Jelly Beans

Chocolate

Basket

Easter Bunny

Easter Eggs

Chick

Bonnet

Day Out

How about a day of fun
out with the other kids?

Swimming
Pool

Binoculars

Pinecone

Treehouse

Tent

Camera

Windmill

Pebbles

Amusement Park

Thrilling rides make a great day at the amusement park.

Toy Car

Carousel

Sky Balloon Ride

Swings

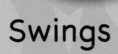

Skee-Ball

Go-Kart

Roller
Coaster

Boat Ride

Water Slide

Whirligig

Bumper
Car

Spring Horse

Ticket Booth

Kiddie Train

Cotton Candy

Ferris Wheel

In the Kitchen

How many of these objects have you seen in your kitchen?

Blender

Whisk

Microwave

Fridge

Oven

Toaster

Kettle

Frying Pan

Food Containers

Kitchen Scales

Knife

Baking Tray

Rolling Pin

Cutting Board

Dishwasher

Juicer

Ladle

In the Office

The office is where people do their work.

Desk

Crayons

Pencil

Sharpener

Computer

Eraser

January 2010

Desk Calendar

Ruler

Armchair

Pen

Pen Stand

Notebook

Hole Punch

Bookshelf

Box File

Stapler

In the Dining Room

You may find all these objects in the room where you have your meals.

Bananas

Fork

Pear

Apple

Strawberries

Butter

Cake

Orange

Place Mat

Plate

Yogurt

Soup Bowl

Salt and
Pepper Shakers

Glass

Napkin
Ring

Napkin
Holder

Napkin

In the Garden

Do you have a garden? Have you seen these objects there before?

Plant

Watering Can

Flowerpot

Wheelbarrow

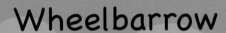

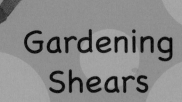

Gardening Gloves

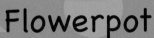

Garden Chair

Gardening Shears

Shovel

Clippers

Rake

Paving Stones

Tree

Flower

Spade

Trowel

Fertilizer

Weeds

Early Vehicles

These are some of the earliest forms of transport used by man.

Longboat

Sedan Chair

Stagecoach

Galley

Buckboard

Buggy

Horse-Drawn Cab

Covered Wagon

Two-Wheelers

The bicycle is not the only machine on two wheels.

Superbike

Cruiser Motorcycle

Scooter

Touring Bike

Moped

Bicycle

Dirt Bike

Street Motorcycle

Cars

There are so many different types of cars.

Go-Kart

Limousine

Estate

Sports Car

4x4 Limousine

Racing Car

Hatchback Car

4x4

Convertible

Dragster

Saloon

Golf Cart

Vintage Car

Mini Car

Dune Buggy

Minibus

Jeep

Working Machines

These machines are used to do different types of work.

Farm Tractor

Combine Harvester

Steamroller

Taxi

Bulldozer

Forklift

Ambulance

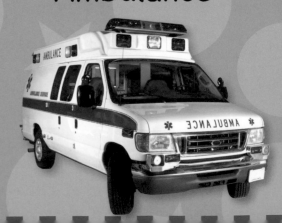

Rock Grader

Airport Tow
Tractor

Digger

Fire Engine

Baggage Train
Tractor

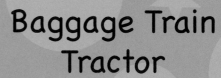

Police Car

Horse-Drawn
Carriage

Lawn
Mower

Garbage Truck

Delivery Van

Trucks & Buses

Have you ever seen so many different kinds of trucks and buses?

Cement Truck

Flatbed Truck

Dump Truck

Car Transporter

Articulated Lorry

Road Train

Tanker Truck

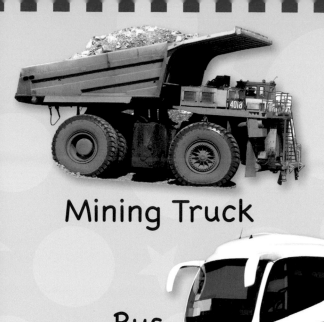

Mining Truck

Tow Truck

Bus

Motor Home

Pickup Truck

Monster Truck

Mini Truck

Trailer Truck

Double-Decker Bus

Delivery Truck

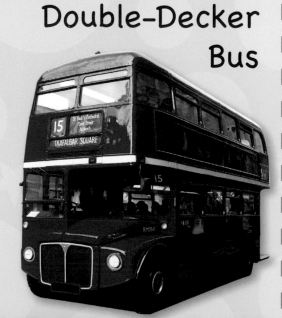

Watercrafts

All these machines move on or below the water.

Cruise Ship

Hovercraft

Kayak

Cargo Ship

Life Raft

Barge

Canoe

Tanker Ship

Rowboat

Submarine

Motorboat

Race Boat

Sailboard

Luxury Boat

Catamaran

Sailboat

Hydrofoil

Aircrafts

High in the sky, that is where you will find these machines.

Glider

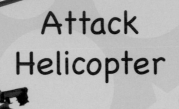

Attack Helicopter

Blimp

Jet

Radar Plane

Bomber

Tanker Plane

Hot Air Balloon

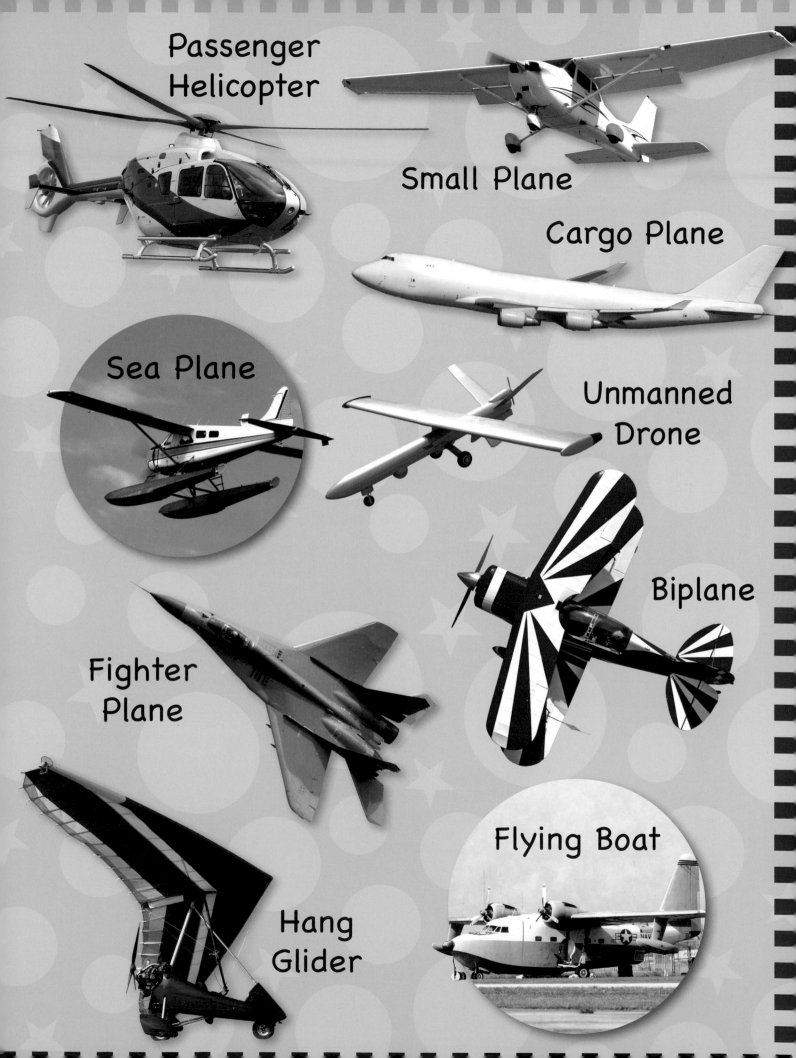

Passenger
Helicopter

Small Plane

Cargo Plane

Sea Plane

Unmanned
Drone

Biplane

Fighter
Plane

Hang
Glider

Flying Boat

Other Vehicles

These machines are all different from the others. Can you tell why?

Rickshaw

Snowmobile

Train Engine

3000

Space Shuttle

Tricycle

Autorickshaw

25

Segway

25

Amphibious
Vehicle

Stroller

Monorail

Skateboard

Scooter

Quad

Sled

Rocket

Tram

Jet Ski

How I Feel

We all have feelings and express them all the time.

Blushing

Excited

Wink

Surprised

Happy

Shy

Bored

Upset

Lonely

Playful

Sad

Scared

Tired

Angry

Teary

Scowl

Hurt

Musical Instruments

Everybody loves music. Listening to music is a soothing experience.

Flute

Thumb Piano

Harmonica

Accordion

Tambourine

Mandolin

Drums

Indian Tabla Drums

Saxophone

Maracas

Clarinet

Acoustic Guitar

Violin

Banjo

Piano

Ocarina

Carved African Djembe

Sports

Playing a sport is not just fun, it is also good for your health.

Beach Volleyball

Swimming

High Jump

Football

Long Jump

Cricket

Basketball

Tennis

Soccer

Squash

Golf

Table Tennis

Bowling

Gymnastics

Volleyball

Running

Croquet

Games We Play

And now it's time for some fun and games with friends.

Skipping

Follow the Leader

Patty-Cake

Backgammon

Cowboys and Indians

Checkers

Jigsaw Puzzles

Hopscotch

Chess

Hide-and-Seek

Frisbee

Rock, Paper, Scissors

Tag

Tic-Tac-Toe

Marbles

Leapfrog

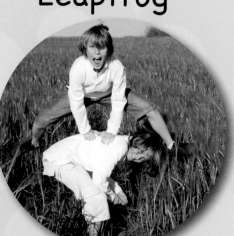

Catch

Descriptive Words

These words tell you what something looks or feels like.

Soft

Small

Hard

Big

Hot

Tall

Short

Cold

Tall

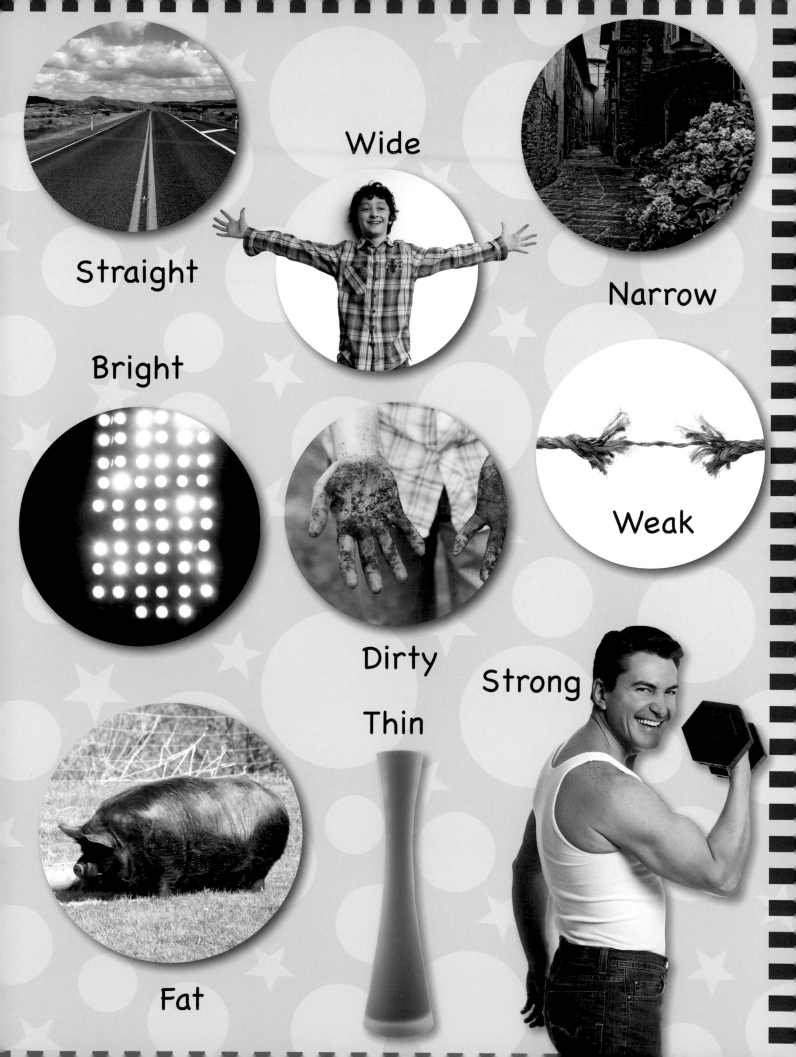

Straight

Wide

Narrow

Bright

Weak

Dirty

Strong

Thin

Fat

In the School

These objects you may find in your school.

Cafeteria

Locker

Paintbrush

Teacher

Schooldesk

Schoolbag

Flipchart

Lunch Box

Trash Can

Notice Board

Notebook

Textbooks

Water Bottle

Globe

Chalk

Blackboard

Clothing Accessories

Accessories are used with clothes and help us look good.

Handbag

Tie Pin

String Tie

Necktie

Mirror

Cufflinks

Watch

Bow
Tie

Hair Brush

Coin Purse

Glasses

Headband

Neckerchief

Barrette

Umbrella

Ribbon

Wallet

Fruits

Everybody loves fruits. They are so juicy and delicious.

Cherry

Pineapple

Melon

Grape

Grapefruit

Raspberry

Peach

Blueberry

Watermelon

Plum

Fig

Kiwi

Guava

Mango

Lemon

Pomegranate

Apricot

Papaya

Vegetables

Vegetables are good for health.
You should eat your vegetables.

Carrot

Cucumber

Cabbage

Turnip

Spinach

Asparagus

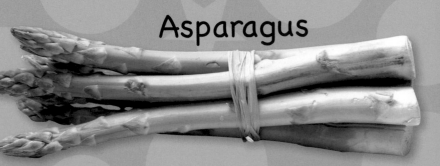

Bell Pepper

Broccoli

Celery

Radish

Peas

Lettuce

Cauliflower

Beetroot

Onion

Potato

Spices We Use

Food tastes good when we add spices to give it flavor.

Coriander

Paprika

Star Anise

Cloves

Fennel

Cardamom

Mint

Oregano

Ginger

Salt

Bay Leaves

Sage

Garlic

Nutmeg

Black Pepper

Saffron

Parsley

Sweets We Eat

Do you have a sweet tooth? Then you will love these sweets.

Mousse

Cupcake

Pie

Jelly

Lollipop

Meringues

Fudge

Fruit Tart

Sweet Butter
Fudge

Custard

Jelly Beans

Swiss Roll

Macarons

Brownie

Chocolate Chip
Cookies

Sweets

Cream Puffs

Drinks

What do you like to drink on a hot day? Do you like these drinks?

Cola

Cranberry Juice

Buttermilk

Apple Juice

Iced Coffee

Water

Smoothie

Lemonade

Ginger Ale

Orange Juice

Carrot Juice

Tomato Juice

Milk Shake

Coffee

Hot Chocolate

Tea

Iced Tea

Foods We Eat

What is your favorite food?
Do you like any of these?

Sushi

Fajita

Pasta

Cheeseburger

Soup

Corn-on-the-Cob

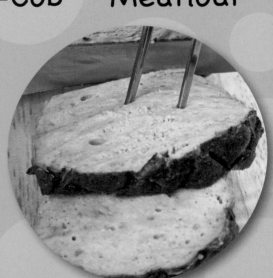
Meatloaf

Pancakes

Lasagna

Taco

Salad

Fish and Chips

Bacon Roll

Curry

Pizza

Fried Rice

Steak

Snacks

Feeling hungry? How about a tasty snack?

Bagel

Chips

Croissant

Crackers

Energy Bar

Doughnuts

Hot Dog

Sandwich

Nachos

Pretzel

Nuts

Quiche

Waffles

Marshmallows

Raisins

Wafers

Popcorn

Condiments

These products help make our food taste better. Ketchup, anyone?

Pickle

Honey

Vinegar

Salad Dressing

Ketchup

Olive Oil

Soy Sauce

Chocolate Sauce

Jam

Chilli Sauce

Mustard

Marmalade

Sour Cream

Barbeque
Sauce

Mayonnaise

Cheese Spread

Salsa

Flowers

Everybody loves flowers. They are so colorful and sweet smelling.

Forget-Me-Not

Rose

Lotus

Foxglove

Lily

Chrysanthemum

Sunflower

Tulip

Daffodil

Primrose

Bird of Paradise

Orchid

Iris

Dahlia

Daisy

Crocus

People We Meet

How many of these people have you met lately?

Fisherman

Blacksmith

Doctor

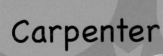

Carpenter

Cobbler

Engineer

Fireman

Farmer

Astronaut

Hair Dresser

Doorman

Chef

Bellboy

Grocery clerk

Butler

Chauffeur

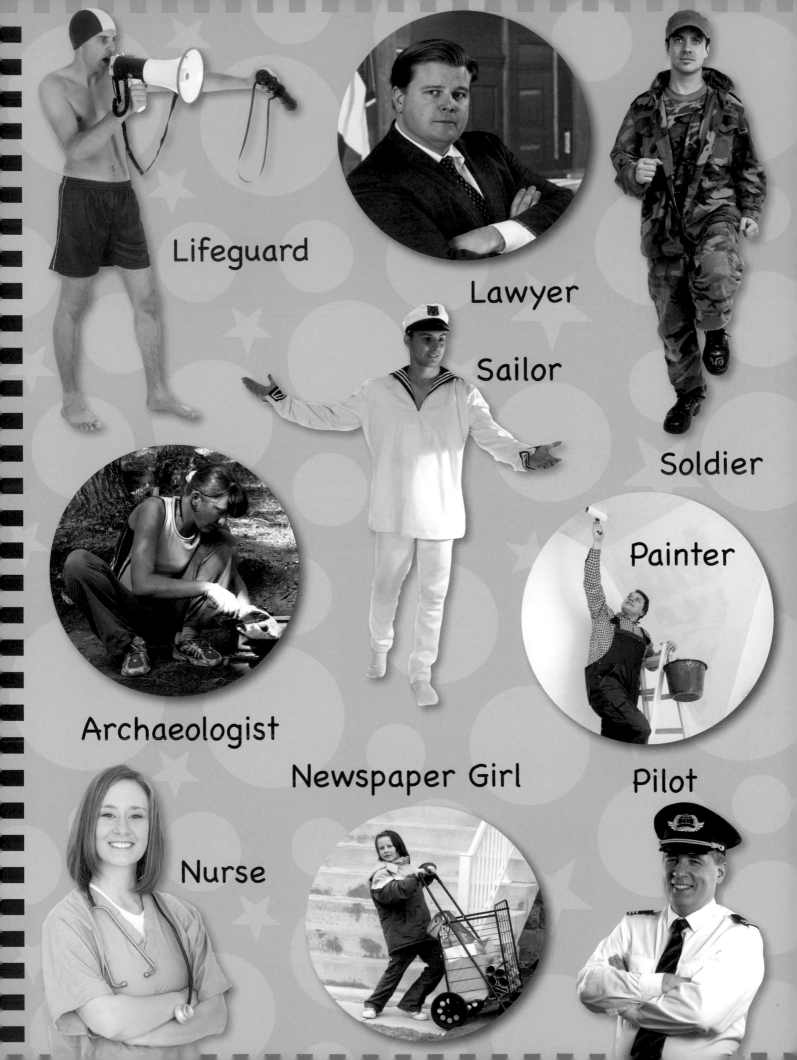

Lifeguard

Lawyer

Sailor

Soldier

Painter

Archaeologist

Newspaper Girl

Pilot

Nurse

Tailor

Sculptor

Maid   Postman

Electrician

Security Guard

Vet

Builder

Beautician

Places We Go

These are some of the places you may visit for different reasons.

Mall

Cinema

Amusement Park

Bookshop

School
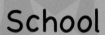

Supermarket

Library

Swimming Pool

Restaurant

Delicatessen

Park

Arcade

Laundromat

Zoo

Museum

Clothes Store

Toy Store

Story Characters

What are your favorite characters? What do you like reading about?

Castle

Prince

Magician

King

Dragon

Monster

Princess

Wizard

Mermaid

Troll

Unicorn

Pony

Fairy

Ballerina

Knight

Cowboy

Things to Do

How many of these activities do you do?

Hug

Lie Down

Dance

Shout

Sit

Drive

Shake Hands

Run

Play Fight

Whisper

Sing

Kick

Kiss

Walk

Wave

Stand

Push

My Tools

These are some of the tools your parents might use around the house.

Saw

Hammer

Nuts

Hacksaw

Scissors

Measuring Tape

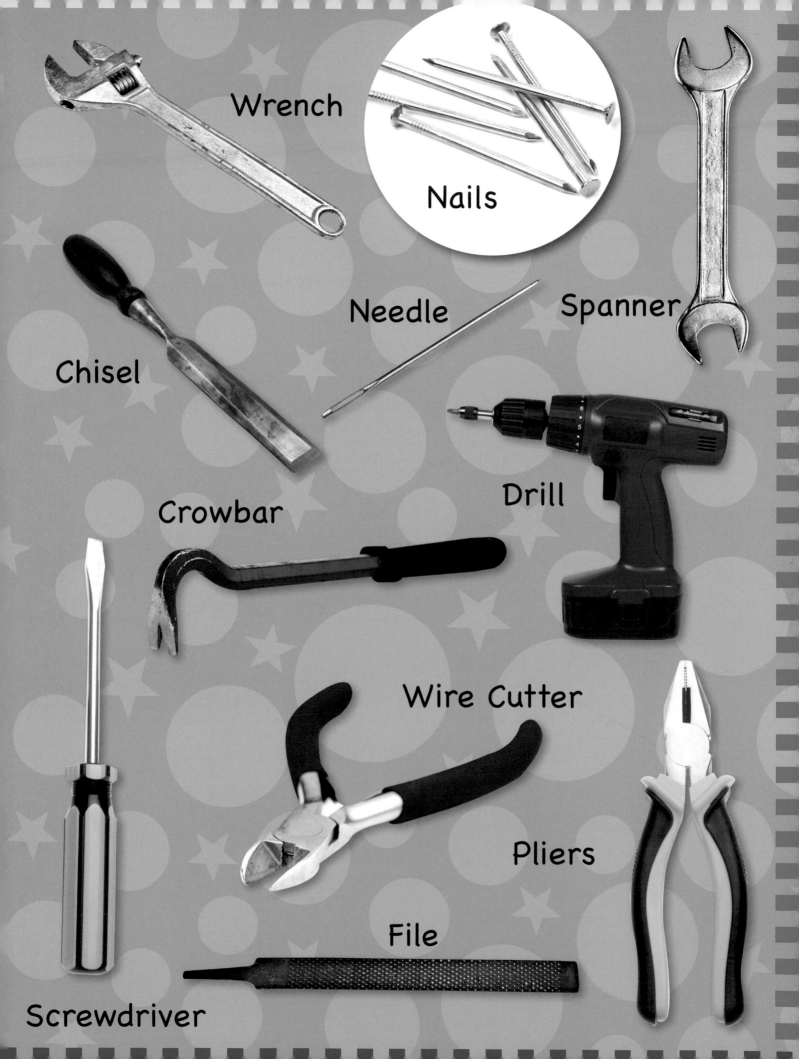

Wrench

Nails

Spanner

Chisel

Needle

Crowbar

Drill

Wire Cutter

Pliers

File

Screwdriver

Baby Animals

What do you think these baby animals will grow up to be?

Cygnet

Foal

Kitten

Joey

Duckling

Chick

Piglet

Kid

Puppy

Lion Cub

Fawn

Calf

Lamb

Tadpole

Alligator
Hatchling

Rabbit Kit

Gosling

Valuables

All these things are precious and expensive. Be careful with them.

Coins

Coral

Emerald

Opal

Garnet

Gold

Pearl

Amber

Dollar
Bills

Platinum

Silver

Diamond

Turquoise

Ruby

Jade

Topaz

Sapphire

Jewelry

Lots of people wear jewelry.

Pendant

Necklace

Earring

Anklet

Locket

Hair Clip

Tiara

Bracelet

Amulet

Brooch

Hair Pin

Bangle

Hair Sticks

Ring

Toe Ring

Choker

Shapes

These are some of the common shapes you will find around you.

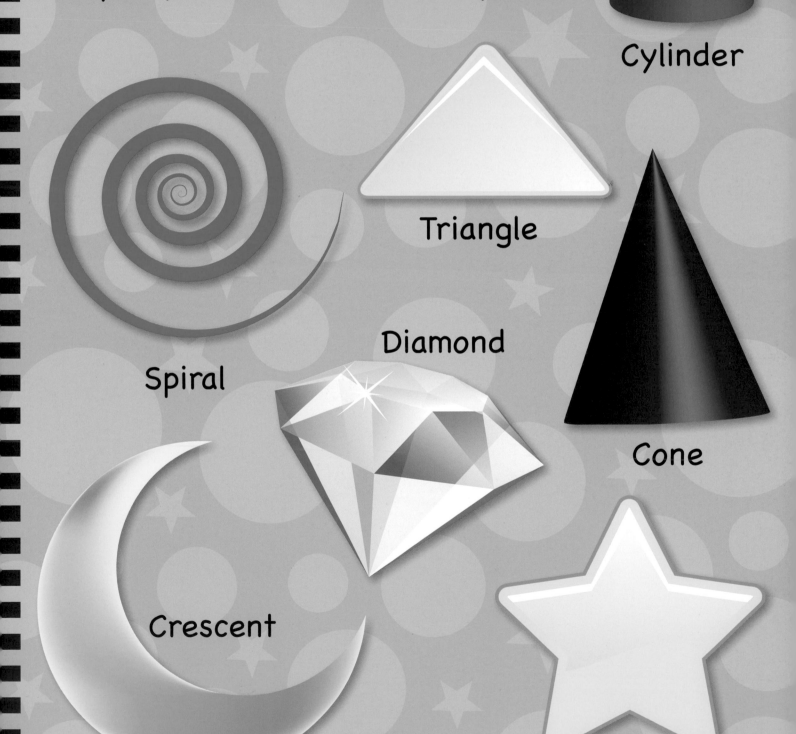

Cylinder

Spiral

Triangle

Diamond

Cone

Crescent

Star

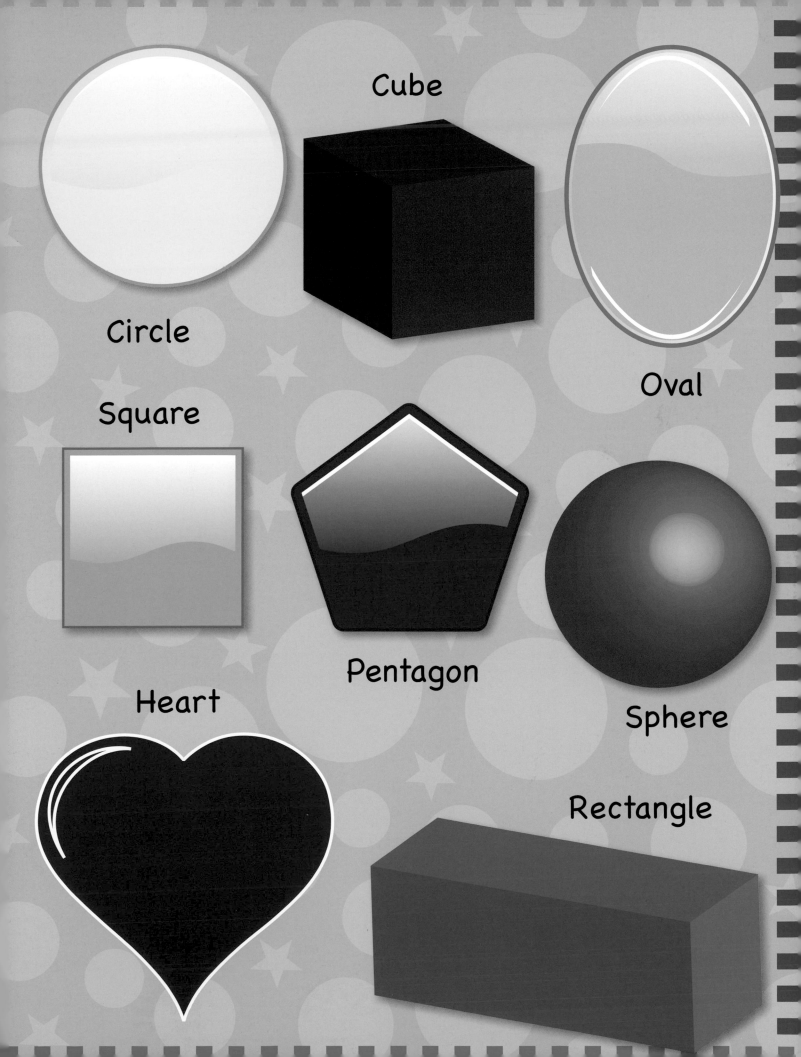

Circle

Cube

Oval

Square

Pentagon

Sphere

Heart

Rectangle